Learning
DISCARD
about
Bees
from
Mr. Krebs

written by
ALICE K. FLANAGAN

**photographs by
CHRISTINE OSINSKI**

Reading Consultant
LINDA CORNWELL
**Learning Resource Consultant
Indiana Department of Education**

CHILDREN'S PRESS® *A Division of Grolier Publishing*
New York • London • Hong Kong • Sydney • Danbury, Connecticut

*To Dale, who was my teacher,
and to Laurie for her patience.
—William Krebs*

*Special thanks to William Krebs
for allowing us to tell his story.*

Visit Children's Press® on the Internet at:
http://publishing.grolier.com

Library of Congress Cataloging-in-Publication Data
Flanagan, Alice K.
    Learning about bees from Mr. Krebs / written by Alice K. Flanagan ;
photographs by Christine Osinski ; reading consultant, Linda Cornwell.
        p. cm. – (Our neighborhood)
    Summary: Follows a beekeeper as he raises honeybees in hives in his
backyard, uses special care in handling the bees, and jars their sweet
honey to share with family and friends.
    ISBN 0-516-21136-6 (lib. bdg.)   0-516-26539-3 (pbk.)
    1. Bee culture—Juvenile literature. 2. Honeybee—Juvenile litera-
ture. 3. Beekeepers—Juvenile literature. [1. Beekeepers. 2.
Occupations. 3. Bee culture. 4. Honeybee.] I. Osinski, Christine, ill.
II. Title. III. Series: Our neighborhood (New York, N.Y.)
SF523.5.F53 1999
638'.1—dc21   98-44691
                                                         CIP
                                                         AC

Photographs ©: Christine Osinski

© 1999 by Alice K. Flanagan and Christine Osinski
All rights reserved. Published simultaneously in Canada
Printed in the United States of America
1 2 3 4 5 6 7 8 9 10 R 08 07 06 05 04 03 02 01 00 99

It's spring! Busy honeybees are gathering food from the flowers in Mr. Krebs's garden.

Mr. Krebs is a beekeeper. He raises honeybees in large wooden boxes called hives.

Twenty-two years ago Mr. Krebs's friend taught him how to care for honeybees.

Now, Mr. Krebs is teaching his grandson Gib those important things.

First, he makes sure Gib wears the
special clothing that protects him
from bee stings.

Next, they check the hives to see
if the bees are healthy.

Sometimes, Mr. Krebs covers the hives with smoke to calm the bees.

Honeybees are important insects. They make honey that is delicious to eat.

They make wax that we use to make candles. And they help many plants grow.

There are many wooden frames
inside a hive. On each frame, the
bees build little cells, called combs,
from wax.

The frame together with the combs is called a honeycomb. This is where the bees lay eggs and store honey.

Honeybees live in large groups called colonies. Each bee has a different job to do for the colony.

14

Some of the bees leave the hive to gather food from flowers. At each flower, they collect pollen and a sweet juice called nectar.

As the bees fly from one flower to another, they leave some of the pollen behind. This is called pollination. Many fruits and vegetables need pollination to grow.

When the bees return to the hive
with nectar, they turn it into honey.

Each year, in the fall,
Mr. Krebs takes honey
from the hives.

First, he removes some of the honeycombs.

He uses a hot knife to melt the wax caps covering the combs. Later, he will melt the wax and make candles.

Then, Mr. Krebs puts the honeycombs into a machine.

21

He spins
the
machine,

and the honey drips down into a
container.

Mr. Krebs fills jars with the honey.

He sells some of the honey at neighborhood fairs. He gives the rest to his family and friends.

Mr. Krebs takes only a little honey
from the hives because the bees
need a lot of food during the winter.

If the bees' supply of honey gets low, Mr. Krebs makes "candy" for them. He mixes sugar and syrup together. Then he pours it into thin squares.

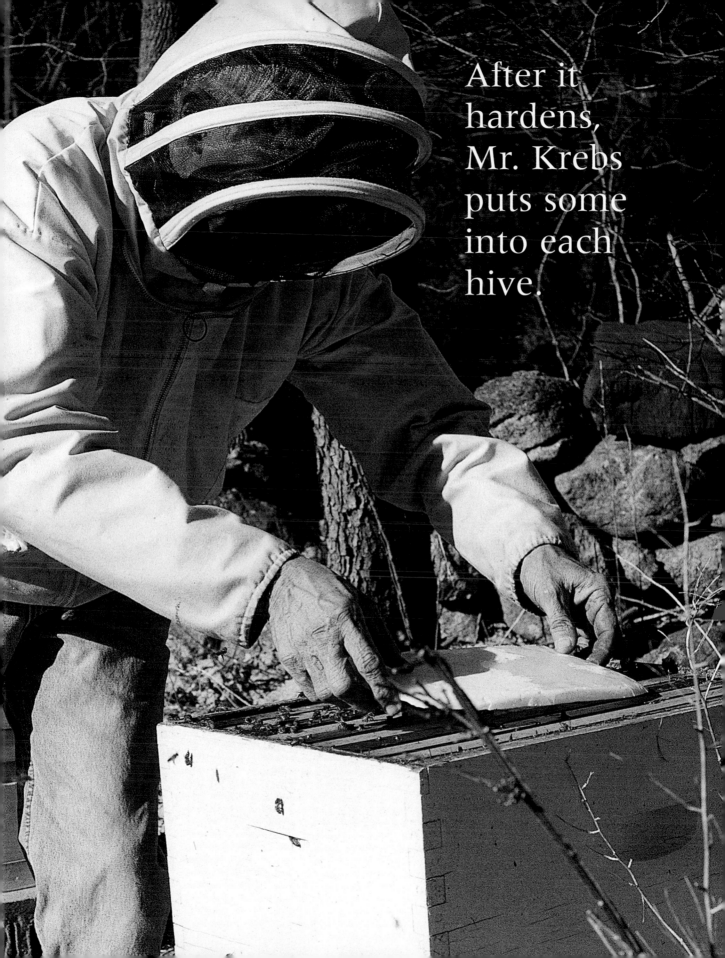

After it hardens, Mr. Krebs puts some into each hive.

Mr. Krebs is a good beekeeper and
teacher. He teaches Gib and other
school children about how bees live.

It is fun to learn about honeybees
from Mr. Krebs!

Meet the Author
and the Photographer

Alice Flanagan and Christine Osinski are sisters. They grew up together telling stories and drawing pictures in a brown brick bungalow in a southwest-side neighborhood of Chicago, Illinois. Today they write stories and take photographs professionally.

Ms. Flanagan resides in Chicago with her husband and works as a freelance writer. Ms. Osinski is a photographer and teaches at The Cooper Union for the Advancement of Science and Art in New York City. She lives with her husband and two sons in Ridgefield, Connecticut.